ALL THE COLORS OF ME

PICTURING MY GRATITUDE

KNOWING AND SHOWING MY FEELINGS THROUGH ART

ANNA SHEPHERD
illustrated by ALICIA MÁS

PowerKiDS press

Published in 2027
by The Rosen Publishing Group, Inc.
2544 Clinton Street, Buffalo, NY 14224

First published in Great Britain in 2023 by Hodder & Stoughton

Credits

Series Editor: Grace Glendinning

Series Designer: Alicia Más

Illustrations: Alicia Más

Cataloging-in-Publication Data

Names: Shepherd, Anna, author. | Más, Alicia, illustrator.
Title: Picturing my gratitude / Anna Shepherd, illustrated by Alicia Más.
Description: Buffalo, New York : PowerKids Press, 2027. | Series: All the colors of me
Identifiers: ISBN 9781499458763 (pbk.) | ISBN 9781499458770 (library bound) | ISBN 9781499458787 (ebook)
Subjects: LCSH: Gratitude in children--Juvenile literature. | Gratitude--Juvenile literature.
Classification: LCC BF723.G7 S547 2027 | DDC 179.9--dc23

Printed in China

CPSIA Compliance Information: Batch #QS27PK. For further information contact Rosen Publishing at 1-800-237-9932.

CONTENTS

LISTENING TO GRATITUDE 4
ART-MAKING CAN HELP 6
GRATITUDE IS ... 8
GRATITUDE FEELS LIKE 10
GRATITUDE LOOKS LIKE 12
GRATITUDE ACTS LIKE 14
MANY SHADES OF GRATITUDE 16
SPEAKING OF GRATITUDE 18
CAN'T FIND THE GRATITUDE? 20
PRACTICING GRATITUDE 22
YOU ARE A GRATITUDE ARTIST! 24

KEY TERMS AND FURTHER RESOURCES 28
A GUIDE FOR ADULTS 30
HELPFUL CONTACTS 32

LISTENING TO GRATITUDE

This book is about moments when something sparks our thankfulness and positivity. Those moments often lead to a feeling called gratitude.

Can you think of something or someone you feel grateful for right now? A good friend, a kind teacher, a sunny day?

As you think about it, start to look inside you to see where the gratitude clues are ...

The amazing thing is, we can always <u>grow</u> our positivity and feel this lovely feeling even more often!

The more we try it out, the more we start spotting things to be thankful for and the happier we feel about our lives.

Knowing and showing our gratitude can also make others feel happier. Being grateful is good for us and everyone around us.

ART-MAKING CAN HELP

Creativity is a wonderful tool to help us explore gratitude.

Words can sometimes float away or might not say exactly what you want them to. With your art, you can capture gratitude on the paper and keep or share it!

PLAYING WITH COLORS AND ENJOYING WHATEVER ENDS UP ON THE PAPER CAN LEAD TO GRATITUDE ALL BY ITSELF, TOO!

When I look at the sea and the sky, I feel its amazingness in my body and mind.
I can't find the words, but making a picture can show my big feelings.

You might think, "But I'm no good at art!" (Impossible!) But you don't have to worry about what it will look like.
It is all about DOING. Then we see how the DOING helps us understand our feelings.

So let's get creative and see what happens!

GRATITUDE IS …

… when we think about and celebrate what is good in our lives.

Try thinking about things in the world that are awesome and cost no money at all – stars, rainbows, laughing with friends, music …

Some of these are so "normal," we can forget to notice them, day after day.

But looking out for the **good** can help us feel **happier** and more optimistic. Noticing what we DO have, rather than what we DON'T can really increase our gratitude.

Babies look at everything with amazement – everything in the world is new to them!

Pretend to be like a toddler – look at a leaf, a bug, a flower, or anything at all and pretend you are seeing it for the **first time.**

You could draw a picture of the things you have noticed. Do you look at these things differently if you imagine you are looking with the eyes of a baby?

Put up your Thankful Details poster somewhere you will see it every day.

The WORLD is INCREDIBLE. Sometimes we just need to remind ourselves!

Doing art is a fun way to understand and show what your

GRATITUDE FEELS LIKE.

Gather some paper and crayons.

Let's begin by thinking about all the people and things that have helped you to be able to make art today.

With a feeling of gratitude, spend a moment using all your senses to appreciate your piece of paper – smell it, touch it, and look at it – every bit of it.

Now do the same with the crayons.

Aren't our senses amazing? Do you ever stop and say a big thank you? Try it now, and as you think about your gratitude, draw yourself some reminders.

THANK YOU, SENSES!

How does your body feel when you are in the middle of making some art? Does it feel a bit like gratitude or like something else? Notice those feelings when they come around!

Art can help us hold up a mirror to see what our

GRATITUDE LOOKS LIKE.

Spend a moment filling yourself up with gratitude.

Notice how it feels inside and then look in a mirror to see how it looks on the outside.

Are you smiling? Tearful? Standing a bit taller? Feeling warm or relaxed? What are your eyes doing?

Draw these details in a Gratitude Self-Portrait.

IT MIGHT BE HELPFUL TO LOOK AT IT NEXT TIME YOU FEEL A BIT FED UP.

Now think of gratitude itself as a creature. What would it look like?

Would it be fluffy or smooth?
How big would it be?
What kind of face do you imagine?
How about its voice?

Have fun designing it.

How about writing a story about your new imaginary gratitude friend? Can the creature help someone find their lost thankfulness?

Sharing and showing our gratitude is a huge part of its strength. So, let's get to know what your

GRATITUDE ACTS LIKE.

Sometimes it's hard to spot the good things when everything seems to be going wrong, but there is always something to be grateful for.

Think of it as a little glimmer of color to begin with.

If you start looking out for these glimmers, you'll soon notice more and more of them. Imagine a simple walk that fills you right to the top with joy!

Acts of kindness are a great way to show and share this thankfulness. The happy feelings will grow for everyone – the one who says thanks and the one who is thanked.

Why not help the teacher clean up in class, or help out at home? What about giving a handmade gift or sharing some food you've made?

Pay attention to your difficult feelings—they are telling you something and need looking after. However, by seeking out gratitude whenever we can, we might feel stronger when facing the hard stuff.

Looking back at your life so far can give you a lovely picture of your

MANY SHADES OF GRATITUDE.

Let's make a Gratitude Lifeline.

Draw a line on a big piece of paper. At one end write "ME AS A BABY" and at the other end write "NOW."

At different places along the line, draw things that you have felt grateful for at different times in your life. Here are some examples from my life, to inspire you!

* When a friend invited me to their party
* When a doctor helped fix my broken leg
* When I got a part in a play
* When I finally learned to ride a bike, swim, read ...

I THINK YOUR PAPER MIGHT GET PRETTY FULL UP!

Now for a challenge: think of something that happened in the past that you didn't feel grateful for at the time, but are thankful for now.

Fit these along your lifeline if you can!

It's amazing how we can go from grumpy to grateful when thinking about the exact same thing!

SPEAKING OF GRATITUDE

might seem easy, but sometimes we feel a bit shy or awkward saying our feelings out loud.

Just as with most things, practicing in a safe way first can help us feel braver later! Let's do some creative role-playing.

You might want to practice this as a play with a friend, or draw it as a comic strip to read aloud.

Can you think of someone you would like to say thank you to now?

You could write them a letter of gratitude or draw them a picture to show them how you feel.

How about delivering it by hand or by mail – it will make both of you feel good inside.

Keep finding more moments in your day when you can say or show thanks.

We've looked at lots of ways to feel grateful, but what if you just

CAN'T FIND THE GRATITUDE?

You can't always be happy. Sometimes, it just feels impossible to look on the bright side of life.

It can make you feel even worse if you tell yourself you must be thankful when you are not feeling it deep down inside.

It is important to take care of your sad or scared feelings, but remember you don't have to do it alone.

Perhaps getting the feelings out and onto paper can help you think about them in a new way?

The problem might even feel a bit different, maybe a bit smaller, once you get it out of your head and share the weight of it with a loved one.

With shrinking worries, there may be more space in your head, and you might have room for some gratitude, too! And some fun!

IMPORTANT: We must never accept being hurt or treated badly. Speak to a trusted adult if you need some extra help to deal with big worries or sadness.

PRACTICING GRATITUDE

can help prepare you for when you need your gratitude skills the most!

Have a go at writing an illustrated Gratitude Journal before you head to bed each night.

If you add to it every night, it can fill your head with positive thoughts and maybe even help you to have a good night's sleep.

Why not decorate the pages with some images that capture your grateful feelings?

What about spending the day taking photos of all the amazing things in your world?

How can you photograph them to capture the wonderful ways they make you thankful?

With permission, print and pin up your photography in a place where you can see the images often and feel a big wave of gratitude!

YOU ARE A GRATITUDE ARTIST!

By now you've probably done lots of thankfulness art. How do you feel seeing all your creativity?

Here are even more ideas to help you grow your gratitude.

With a trusted adult, head outside and make some art with things you find in nature. Say thank you to all that the world gives you for free.

(But don't disturb living plants or wildlife! Only use what has fallen on the ground.)

YOU CAN ALSO TAKE THE TREASURE HUNT INSIDE!

With permission, try gathering materials that you like the look and feel of. Maybe they are soft or fluffy? Or how about sparkly sequins and smooth old buttons?

Make a collage of your precious findings.

Pay attention to your response to each texture and color – we can say thanks for the many beautiful things around us as we make beautiful art.

Try this gratitude exercise and see if it increases your happiness.

Every night for three weeks write down three things that you feel thankful for and put them in a Gratitude Jar. You can look back and see how many things you have thought of.

You could gather twigs or use paper to make a Gratitude Tree.

Cut out lots of paper leaves. Every time you notice something you feel thankful for, write it on a leaf and add it to your tree. It will be lovely watching your tree blossom.

Art does not have to be realistic. You can always explore your shades of gratitude through playing with colors and shapes.

Close your eyes and think about a time when you felt grateful for someone or something in your life.

Really notice how thinking of this feels in your body.

Can you make a picture that shows each feeling? What colors, shapes, lines, and textures will you choose?

SOMEONE WHO REALLY LISTENED TO YOU

A HUG

A PLACE OR THING THAT MEANT A LOT

KIND WORDS

KEY TERMS

Celebrate: to do something special or enjoyable for an important event; to praise or notice that someone or something is important.

Creativity: using your imagination to create something.

Glimmer: a faint sign of a feeling or thing.

Gratitude: thankfulness for things in your life.

Inspire: fill with the urge to do something.

Optimistic: feeling hopeful and confident about the future.

Positivity: the act of thinking of the good things about a situation rather than the bad ones.

Precious: something of great value.

Shades: slightly different varieties of something, such as a color.

Texture: the feel or look of the surface of something.

BOOKS TO READ

***Kids Can Cope* series,**
by Gill Hasson (Franklin Watts)

- *Bounce Back from Disappointment*
- *Face Your Fears*
- *Let Go of Jealousy*
- *Put Your Worries Away*
- *Say Hi When You're Shy*
- *Step Back from Frustration*
- *Take Charge of Anger*
- *Turn Away from Teasing*

***A World Full of Feelings* series,**
by Louise Spilsbury (Franklin Watts)

- *Finding Calm*
- *Finding Courage*
- *Finding Happiness*
- *Finding Kindness*

***Build Resilience* series,**
by Honor Head (Franklin Watts)

- *Anxiety and Self-Esteem*
- *Coping with Change*
- *Friendships and Bullying*
- *Unexpected Challenges*

WEBSITES to **VISIT** with the help of an adult:

Headspace.com

A website and app offering meditation and mindfulness tools to expand on the practice of understanding and dealing with emotions.

Youthmindfulness.org

Resources for mindfulness programs for young people.

HOW TO USE THIS BOOK: A GUIDE FOR ADULTS

This series of art therapy books has been developed to provide a creative starting point for further discussion and exploration around children's emotions.

Each book is intended for children to **share** with trusted adults, whether one-on-one or in a group setting in the classroom or elsewhere.

This book, *Picturing My Gratitude*, is an exploration of the look and feel of thankfulness. When dealing with any emotion, big or small, the utmost priority is making children feel **safe and heard** as they think things through.

Whether sharing at home or in a group setting, plan to begin at a time when you and your child or group are relaxed and have an uninterrupted moment to share an activity. It is important that the adult leading the activity is emotionally available when sitting to do this. This can be hard when you feel rushed and stressed, so choose the timing carefully.

Only you will know how much time and energy you and your child or group are able to give to this practice in each session, and what will suit your setting - dip in; read it completely; return to it again at times in the future. No matter what, **don't push things** - try out the bits that your child or group are most drawn to. Have a go at different activities when they feel right for the progression of the individual or group. Use each approach at a time and place that is **most helpful**.

The activities are catalysts for conversations about how children feel. Once the creativity starts flowing, the session may well grow beyond what's in these pages. Maybe a child has their own ideas about ways to feel a bit better that they could share with you or the group? Try to **listen** and not offer unwelcome solutions or critiques. It can be hard when you want to help, but trust that **with love, support, and encouragement,** children can usually find their own way through.

Also, take **notice of your own feelings** and responses as your child or group creates, and be mindful that you are modelling how to manage and regulate emotions. You do not need to get it right all the time; **be kind to yourself**, just as we encourage the children to be throughout this book. Helping children is not always easy.

In a group setting it is very important to make sure every child feels safe to share and participate. Establish a rapport of **support** and **zero judgement** of their art and expression of emotion.

But keep in mind that some children may need to have additional, dedicated help beyond what is appropriate to do on your own in a classroom or group setting. See page 32 for quick-reference contacts if you feel your child or group member needs further professional or anonymous assistance.

If you are concerned that a child is struggling to cope, then it is worth seeking advice from a professional.

American Art Therapy Association
arttherapy.org/art-therapist-locator

Learn more about art therapy and find a trained therapist to continue emotional work with a creative approach.

Find a Warmline
www.warmline.org

Warmlines are confidential, free phone services that offer emotional support to people who just need someone to talk to. Find a Warmline near you here.

Kids Help Phone
1-800-668-6868
kidshelpphone.ca

Kids Help Phone is a Canadian e-mental health service for youths with counselors available 24 hours a day.

National Mental Health Hotline
1-866-903-3787
mentalhealthhotline.org

This free, 24-hour help line connects people in need with caring, knowledgeable, licensed mental health counselors.

Nemours Kids Health
kidshealth.org

This website is full of helpful health resources for parents, kids, teens, and educators.